Habakkuk

'Jonathan Lamb has done an excellent job of making Habakkuk accessible and exciting. The message that God is in control and is enough, even in the most difficult circumstances, rings out loud and clear for the reader today.'

Clare Heath-Whyte, author of First Wives' Club *and* Old Wives' Tales

'We all wrestle with the mysterious purposes of God in our lives and in the lives of those we love. This is the theme of the preaching of Habakkuk. With his usual clarity, warmth and contemporary application, Jonathan Lamb takes us to the heart of this book. Elizabeth McQuoid has adapted Jonathan's material so that it will enrich your daily devotions and warm your heart. I enthusiastically recommend this book.'

Paul Mallard, pastor, Widcombe Baptist Church, Bath, former President, Fellowship of Independent Evangelical Churches, and the author of a number of books

30-DAY DEVOTIONAL

Habakkuk

Jonathan Lamb
with Elizabeth McQuoid

INTER-VARSITY PRESS
36 Causton Street, London SW1P 4ST, England
Email: ivp@ivpbooks.com
Website: www.ivpbooks.com

First published 2018

British Library Cataloguing-in-Publication Data
A catalogue record for this book is available from the British Library.

ISBN: 978–1–78359–652–2
eBook ISBN: 978–1–78359–653–9

Typeset in Great Britain by CRB Associates, Potterhanworth, Lincolnshire
Printed in Great Britain by Ashford Colour Press Ltd, Gosport, Hampshire

Inter-Varsity Press publishes Christian books that are true to the Bible and that communicate the gospel, develop discipleship and strengthen the church for its mission in the world.

IVP originated within the Inter-Varsity Fellowship, now the Universities and Colleges Christian Fellowship, a student movement connecting Christian Unions in universities and colleges throughout Great Britain, and a member movement of the International Fellowship of Evangelical Students. Website: www.uccf.org.uk. That historic association is maintained, and all senior IVP staff and committee members subscribe to the UCCF Basis of Faith.

Preface

Can you guess how many sermons have been preached from the Keswick platform? Almost 6,500!

For over 140 years, the Keswick Convention in the English Lake District has welcomed gifted expositors from all over the world. Our archive is a treasure trove of sermons preached on every book of the Bible.

This series is an invitation to mine that treasure. It takes talks from the Bible Reading series given by well-loved Keswick speakers, past and present, and reformats them into daily devotionals. Where necessary, the language has been updated but, on the whole, it is the message you would have heard had you been listening in the tent on Skiddaw Street. Each day of the devotional ends with a fresh section of application designed to help you apply God's Word to your own life and situation.

Whether you are a Convention regular or have never been to Keswick, this Food for the Journey series is a unique opportunity to study the Scriptures with a Bible teacher by your side. Each book is designed to fit in your jacket pocket or handbag so you can read it anywhere – over the breakfast table, on the commute into work or college, while you are waiting in your car, over your lunch break or in bed at night. Wherever life's journey takes you, time in God's Word is vital nourishment for your spiritual journey.

Our prayer is that these devotionals become your daily feast, a nourishing opportunity to meet with God through his Word. Read, meditate, apply and pray through the Scriptures given for each day, and allow God's truths to take root and transform your life.

If these devotionals whet your appetite for more, there is a 'For further study' section at the end of each book. You can also visit our website at <www.keswickministries.org/resources> to find the full range of books, study guides, CDs, DVDs and mp3s available. Why not order an audio recording of the Bible Reading series to accompany your daily devotional?

Let the word of Christ dwell in you richly.
(Colossians 3:16, ESV)

Introduction
Habakkuk

Who is in control?

The sustained threat from rogue states, international terrorism, violence perpetrated by religious extremists, and the moral confusion arising from liberal views of all kinds begs the question: what is happening to our world?

We sense that we have entered into an era of bewildering uncertainty where no-one is in control. There is a fault line in our world, a deep vulnerability that many people express. And it is not simply to do with global events. Our own personal world often seems out of control as we reel from suffering, family tragedies and unanswered prayers.

The prophet Habakkuk knew God was in control, but, like us, his personal experience seemed to contradict this. His belief did not match his experience, and he wrestled with the tension.

A contemporary of Jeremiah, Habakkuk saw that wickedness and oppression were rife in Judah and couldn't understand why God didn't act. He was even more perplexed when God told him he would use the evil Babylonians to bring judgment on Judah.

The book is a dialogue between the prophet and God. Habakkuk confronts God with his confusion and, in doing so, he expresses the voice of the godly in Judah and he speaks for us. He articulates the questions that believers ask and expresses the certainties we must embrace. His memorable closing doxology is no easy believism or superficial triumphalism. He has made a demanding journey from the bewildered questions of chapter 1 to offering the worship of an individual who has discovered that, when everything is stripped away, God is enough.

Habakkuk invites us to discover the foundations of faith in an uncertain world and join the journey from 'why?' to 'worship'.

Day 1

Read Habakkuk 1:1–11
Key verses: Habakkuk 1:2–3

....

²*How long, L*ORD*, must I call for help,*
  but you do not listen?
Or cry out to you, 'Violence!'
  but you do not save?
³*Why do you make me look at injustice?*
  Why do you tolerate wrongdoing?
Destruction and violence are before me;
  there is strife, and conflict abounds.

'How long?' 'Why?' – these are two questions we often ask.

The prophet Habakkuk was also overwhelmed by these questions. He was living in Jerusalem in the final days of the seventh century BC. Josiah, the great king who discovered the law, had pulled down the pagan altars and restored the temple, but he had been followed by

Jehoiakim, who quickly succeeded in reversing all his good work.

King Jehoiakim built his wonderful palaces, exploiting the people in the process, but showed no repentance. And so the priests, politicians and civil servants took their cue from him. They too became perpetrators of violence and injustice, adding to the moral confusion rather than resolving it (verse 3). No wonder Habakkuk declares, 'The wicked hem in the righteous' (verse 4). The few who did remain faithful to the Word of the Lord were completely surrounded by ungodly behaviour which threatened to snuff out all signs of spiritual life.

Habakkuk watched this terrible moral and spiritual decline set in. God's Word was frozen out, and the law was paralysed (verse 4). Justice was replaced with anarchy. The people were determined to forget what God had said and to live life on their own terms.

But it was not just the sinfulness of the people that brought Habakkuk close to despair, it was also the delay in God's action. It was actually Habakkuk's understanding of God that led him to voice this complaint: 'If what I know about you is true, God, then why aren't you acting? Why the delay?' There is an intensity in verses 2–4, suggesting that the prophet shouts, screams, roars, 'Help,

Lord! Why are you allowing people to drift away? Why are you not intervening?'

These questions were not simply academic. Habakkuk is bewildered and is crying out to God with deeply felt pain. As the novelist Peter de Vries puts it, 'The question mark twisted like a fish hook in the human heart' (*The Blood of the Lamb*, University of Chicago Press, 2005, p. 243).

Are there question marks twisting 'like a fish hook' in your heart? Many of us have unresolved 'why' questions in our lives. We won't always find the answers to perplexing questions this side of eternity. When everything seems out of joint, it is OK to admit your bewilderment. But don't believe Satan's lie that God's apparent silence means he is not interested, or not working on your behalf. Like Habakkuk, lay out your complaint honestly before God. Ask him to help you trust his character and learn to live with unanswered questions and mystery.

Day 2

Read Habakkuk 1:1–11
Key verse: Habakkuk 1:5

....

> ⁵*Look at the nations and watch –*
>   *and be utterly amazed.*
> *For I am going to do something in your days*
>   *that you would not believe,*
>   *even if you were told.*

Sometimes we have particular expectations of how God ought to work in our lives and in our world. We think we know how our prayers should be answered. So it is important to note here what God told Habakkuk: 'Look carefully.'

God's response in verse 5 begins with the word 'Look', which picks up Habakkuk's complaint in verse 3: 'Why do you make me look at injustice?' Habakkuk *was* looking, but he needed a different perspective. He needed to see God's perspective.

God had heard Habakkuk's prayer and in fact was already at work. He was not standing by, indifferent to the prophet's concerns. No, he says, I am already at work if only you had eyes to see it. Verses 6–11, which outline God's plan, describe the devastation the Babylonians were about to bring on God's own people. The Babylonians were guilty of international terrorism, ethnic cleansing and the exercise of ruthless power. This great military power would crush everything in its path. And the Lord was behind the series of devastating events that would change the course of history in Habakkuk's day. He had not abandoned his plans. Judah and all of the nations were still under God's watchful eye, if only Habakkuk could see it.

Do you remember Paul's testimony in Philippians 1? He was confined in prison and, for an activist like Paul, this could have been frustrating in the extreme. But he wrote, 'I want you to know, brothers and sisters, that what has happened to me has actually served to advance the gospel' (Philippians 1:12). Paul may have been imprisoned, but he knew God was at work. Every day one of Caesar's personal bodyguards was chained to him; there were four teams of four soldiers – a captive audience! We know that members of the imperial household became Christians. The gospel was reaching social circles it never would have reached had it not been for Paul's witness, extending right up to Nero himself. Paul also mentions that other Christians were encouraged to speak the Word of God more fearlessly (Philippians 1:14). Paul could see that, however unpromising the situation looked, there was another story: God was at work.

Perhaps you belong to a very small church or are working in a demanding situation. Maybe you live in a country where the church is under enormous pressure, or your personal or family situation exerts what seems like a strongly restrictive influence over all you do. God is not indifferent to your struggles; he does not stand aloof. He is watching over you. Take heart – beneath the surface story of your life there is another more glorious story unfolding; there is the reality of God at work. Ask God to help you take a fresh look at your circumstances and open your eyes to what he is doing.

Day 3

Read Habakkuk 1:1–11
Key verses: Habakkuk 1:6–7

....

> [6] *I am raising up the Babylonians,*
>   *that ruthless and impetuous people,*
> *who sweep across the whole earth*
>   *to seize dwellings not their own.*
> [7] *They are a feared and dreaded people;*
>   *they are a law to themselves*
>   *and promote their own honour.*

Some Christians appear to live as if they were in a *Star Wars* adventure, surrounded by equal and opposite forces of good and evil. If something good happens, God has won that battle. If something bad happens, the devil must have triumphed in that round.

But the Bible teaches that God is always in control, always ultimately sovereign.

In fact, what was so troubling for Habakkuk was that, although the Babylonians were in the driving seat of this great war machine, God was the Commander. God was disciplining his people. They had ignored his justice and so they would be subjected to Babylonian justice. God's people were guilty of perpetuating violence and destruction, so that is what they would receive.

But the Babylonians were not just an instrument under God's sovereign authority; they were also an instrument for God's purposes. These verses underline a very profound truth: God is in control. He even controls the movements of ruthless powers and pagan nations. John Calvin commented on these verses: 'It is not by their own instinct but by the hidden impulse of God . . . God can employ the vices of men in executing his judgments. The wicked are led here and there by the hidden power of God' (*Commentaries on the Twelve Minor Prophets, Volume 4: Habakkuk, Zephaniah, Haggai,* CreateSpace Publishing, 2015, pp. 23–24). It might have seemed that the military prowess of the Babylonians would eventually result in their success, but it was God who had raised them up to fulfil his purposes. God really was in control.

The book of Job underlines this point. God granted permission to Satan to test Job, but God set the boundaries (Job 1:8–12). Exactly the same principle appears in the New Testament. The early Christians were bewildered when Jesus was crucified. In their prayer meeting they state that Herod, Pontius Pilate, the Gentiles and the people of Israel had conspired against Jesus. But then they add, 'They did what your power and will had decided beforehand should happen' (Acts 4:28).

The Babylonians might think they are in control; the British or the Americans or ISIS might think they are in control. But the rise and fall of nations and empires, of dictators and terrorists, is in God's hands.

The Bible often urges us to 'remember', because reflecting on God's faithfulness strengthens our resolve to trust and obey him in our present struggles. Remember and reflect on examples from the Bible and your own life when you have witnessed God's control in difficult times. Thank him that even today he is fulfilling his good purposes for your life. Acknowledge his sovereign control and ask for his help to be obedient during dark days.

Day 4

Read Habakkuk 1:12–17
Key verse: Habakkuk 1:12

....

> ¹²*LORD, are you not from everlasting?*
>   *My God, my Holy One, you will never die.*
> *You, LORD, have appointed them to execute*
>   *judgment;*
>   *you, my Rock, have ordained them to punish.*

Listen to these words by Warren Wiersbe: 'Never doubt in the dark what God has told you in the light' (*Be Comforted*, David C. Cook Publishing, 2009, p. 148).

Habakkuk understood that judgment was necessary for Israel, but he couldn't understand how all the violence and devastation could possibly fulfil God's purposes for righteousness. How would it fulfil God's promise of blessing, and when would it all end?

But, like many of the psalmists and other prophets, Habakkuk set his questions in the context of his certainties and affirmed the foundational truths of the Christian faith. He expressed confidence in:

• God's commitment

He speaks to God in direct and personal terms: 'My God, my Holy One'. He is implying, 'You are the faithful, covenant-keeping God; I belong to you.' That is our confidence too. God will not let go of us. Whatever happens, we belong to him. This security is not dependent on our capacity to believe, but on God's faithful commitment to us.

• God's eternity

'LORD, are you not from everlasting?' God is engaged in history, but he is also above all of its turbulent ebb and flow. Whatever our fears and uncertainties, God is eternal, the Rock, the one stable element in an uncertain world. If things are shaking in our lives or in our world, we must hold on to God's changelessness.

• God's purpose

Habakkuk realizes that the coming Babylonian invasion is something God has ordained. Other prophets, like Ezekiel, Jeremiah and Isaiah, also realized that international events are not random. They are all part of God's sovereign purpose.

Habakkuk didn't ignore his troubling questions. He was realistic about the terrible judgment the Babylonians would bring and he cried out honestly to God. But, crucially, in the midst of it all he affirmed what he knew to be true about God.

When we are in difficult situations, it is very easy for questions and doubts to overwhelm us. We need to remind ourselves of the certainties of God's Word and repeat to ourselves the confident realities we have examined. If we respond as Habakkuk did, even in the blackest moments we will discover that God is our refuge and strength.

'Most of your unhappiness in life is due to the fact that you are listening to yourself instead of talking to yourself' (D. Martyn Lloyd-Jones, *Spiritual Depression*, STL, 1965, p. 20).

Today, as you struggle with perplexing questions and are concerned with all that is going on in the world, rehearse the great certainties of faith. Choose five rock-solid affirmations of faith, write them down, meditate on them and let these truths fill you with confidence in God's sovereignty. For example:

- God has said,
    'Never will I leave you;
        never will I forsake you.'
    (Hebrews 13:5)

- The LORD is my rock, my fortress and my deliverer;
        my God is my rock, in whom I take refuge,
        my shield and the horn of my salvation,
            my stronghold.
    (Psalm 18:2)

- Jesus Christ is the same yesterday and today and
    for ever.
    (Hebrews 13:8)

Day 5

Read Habakkuk 1:12–17
Key verse: Habakkuk 1:13

....

> ¹³ *Your eyes are too pure to look on evil;*
>   *you cannot tolerate wrongdoing.*
> *Why then do you tolerate the treacherous?*
>   *Why are you silent while the wicked*
>   *swallow up those more righteous than*
>   *themselves?*

No doubt you have heard the phrase: 'The cure is worse than the disease.'

This was exactly how the situation appeared to Habakkuk. As a prophet, he understood that judgment was inevitable. His problem was that, instead of God's purposes being advanced, they seemed to be going in exactly the opposite direction.

God seemed to be being inconsistent (verse 13). If he is the God of awesome purity, why does he allow the ruthless Babylonians to do their worst? The suspicion is that if he uses them, he must be like them. The imagery of verses 14–17 underlines their ruthless behaviour. As if fishing with a rod and net, the Babylonians sit beside the stream that God has generously stocked with human fish: 'He gathers them up in his drag-net; and so he rejoices and is glad' (verse 15). Historians tell us that the Babylonians placed hooks into the lower jaw of their captives to lead them along with chains. No wonder Habakkuk is appalled by the brutality.

We too are perplexed at what is happening in our world. Like Habakkuk, we are shocked by the violence. We are also bewildered by personal tragedies, which seem to contradict our understanding of God's character. We can't understand how God can use these present circumstances to fulfil his purposes.

I find my experience of sailing helpful here. Once, when we were in the Sound of Mull in Scotland, the winds rose to almost storm force, but the skipper was determined we would make the journey. We soon learnt how to 'beat against the wind'. This is a manoeuvre whereby you sail in one direction and then tack to travel in another direction, in a sustained zigzag movement. You make very slow progress, but the remarkable thing is this: you are using the winds that are against you to make that progress.

It strikes me that this is also a realistic model of the Christian life. Sometimes we think we must always be riding high on some success-orientated spirituality. But Jesus never promised us that. He did promise that whatever winds and waves are thrown at us, we will still make progress to our destination. God uses even those opposing forces to help us move forward.

Can you believe it? The winds and waves that are battering your life right now can be a means of spiritual progress. Practise 'beating against the wind'. Today, look for opportunities to:

- trust God;
- grow in your knowledge and appreciation of his Word;
- deepen your discipleship relationships with other believers;
- pray more fervently;
- serve him wholeheartedly.

Be confident of this: 'He who began a good work in you will carry it on to completion until the day of Christ Jesus' (Philippians 1:6).

Day 6

Read Habakkuk 2:1–3
Key verse: Habakkuk 2:1

....

> ¹*I will stand at my watch*
> *and station myself on the ramparts;*
> *I will look to see what he will say to me,*
> *and what answer I am to give to this complaint.*

How should we pray when we are riddled with questions and doubts?

Here at the start of chapter 2, Habakkuk is quietly, patiently, listening. It seems a million miles away from the mood of Habakkuk's praying that we observed in chapter 1. He had poured out his heart to God and now he is waiting on God.

It is helpful to see that both aspects of prayer are expressed by the same man. Habakkuk, after honestly communicating his concerns and questions, turns away from every distraction and waits on God. It must have been enormously difficult for him to do that. We should not forget what was happening in Jerusalem at the time, a situation that provoked the sustained refrain of 'violence' and 'injustice'. But it was vital for Habakkuk to step away from the turbulence of the city and of his own heart and mind in order to hear God's still small voice.

Psalm 73 reflects this pattern. The psalmist has similar questions and pours out his complaint: 'Why do the wicked always seem to succeed and the righteous suffer? Why, God, do you allow this to continue?' But then in verses 16–17 we reach the turning point in the psalm:

> When I tried to understand all this,
>   it troubled me deeply
> till I entered the sanctuary of God;
>   then I understood their final destiny.

Like Habakkuk, the psalmist took time to come into God's presence, and it was there that his perspective changed. Perhaps you can identify with some of the questions Habakkuk asked in chapter 1. What is your response to those challenges? Sometimes we live more by the maxim: 'Why pray, when you can worry?' Committing these perplexities to God is one of the most important disciplines in our lives.

How often have you 'waited' on God? When faced with a difficult situation, we tend to agonize over it, talk it through with friends or rush to solve the problem. It is harder to take ourselves off to a quiet place, to enter God's sanctuary and pray, allowing him, if necessary, to change our perspective. Don't let prayer be a last resort. Get rid of the distractions and join with the psalmist:

- Wait for the LORD;
     be strong and take heart
     and wait for the LORD.
   (Psalm 27:14)

- I wait for your salvation, LORD,
     and I follow your commands.
   (Psalm 119:166)

- I wait for the LORD, my whole being waits,
     and in his word I put my hope.
   (Psalm 130:5)

Day 7

Read Habakkuk 2:1–3
Key verse: Habakkuk 2:1

....

> ¹*I will stand at my watch*
> *and station myself on the ramparts;*
> *I will look to see what he will say to me,*
> *and what answer I am to give to this complaint.*

When you pray or read the Bible, are you expectant that God will speak?

Here Habakkuk describes himself as someone standing on the ramparts, keeping watch above the city of Jerusalem. He is waiting expectantly for God to speak. You may remember the sense of expectancy in Jerusalem some years later, when Ezra stood in the city centre and read from the Book of the Law. The account is recorded in Nehemiah 8. God's people had returned from exile and had rebuilt the walls of the city. Now, as they prepared for their new life back home, they were desperate to hear and obey the Word of the Lord. Their eagerness and expectancy are expressed in the fact that 'all the people listened attentively' (8:3), and in the way they stood up when the book was opened and bowed down in worship as they came into God's presence. They were ready to hear and respond (Nehemiah 8:1–12).

There is little to be gained from reading the Bible without that kind of expectancy. Jesus' own ministry was frustrated when there was no expectancy on the part of his hearers. He began to teach in the synagogue and he was met by cynicism and incredulity. Expectant faith is the soil in which God's Word will bear fruit, and this is an element in our spiritual life that we need to nurture.

It is one of the lessons from Habakkuk chapter 1. Although he felt the weariness of it all (1:2), Habakkuk kept on praying with perseverance and expectant faith, believing that God would finally speak his Word. Don Carson offers some very useful advice: 'Pray until you pray . . . Christians should pray long enough and honestly enough at a single session to get past the feeling of formalism and unreality that attends a little praying. Many of us in our praying are like nasty little boys who ring front door bells and run away before anyone answers' (*A Call to Spiritual Reformation*, IVP, 1992, pp. 36–37).

Will you 'pray until you pray'?

How would you describe your spiritual posture as you read the Bible and pray? God wants us to be like watchmen on a rampart, waiting expectantly for what he will say. The psalmist uses another image:

> As the deer pants for streams of water,
>   so my soul pants for you, my God.
> My soul thirsts for God, for the living God.
> (Psalm 42:1–2)

Today, spend unhurried time in God's presence, listening for his voice and cultivating that sense of expectancy. Acknowledge that God's Word alone sustains you. Be willing to 'do whatever he tells you' (John 2:5), and 'pray until you pray'.

Day 8

Read Habakkuk 2:1–3
Key verse: Habakkuk 2:1

....

> [1] *I will stand at my watch*
>   *and station myself on the ramparts;*
> *I will look to see what he will say to me,*
>   *and what answer I am to give to this complaint.*

Nobody enjoys being rebuked, but sometimes it is necessary.

Habakkuk was aware of how bold he had been in God's presence in chapter 1 and knew that a rebuke was in order. He says, 'I will look to see what he will say to me, and what answer I am to give to this complaint' (2:1). But there is an alternative reading which says, 'what to answer when I am rebuked'. Or it could also read, 'I will look to see what he will say to me and the correction that I am going to receive.' It is almost shocking to see the way in which he addresses God with his complaints and his anxious questions, and so now, as he stands on the city ramparts, he realizes he must be prepared for the Lord's rebuke, 'the correction that I am going to receive'. He has presented all of the arguments, so now he is submissive enough to wait for the Lord's reproof and discipline.

David Prior rightly observes that 'God looks not just for honesty but he also looks for humility' (*The Message of Joel, Micah and Habakkuk,* IVP, 1988, p. 233). In all prayer we must be submissive as well as honest, ready for what God is going to say to us and open to any reproof or discipline that may be necessary.

Maybe you have heard the story of an announcement that appeared in a missionary magazine concerning the former General Director of a particular mission agency who was retiring, but was going to continue to serve the Lord 'in an advisory capacity'! We are not the ones with the answers when it comes to praying. We are not in control. Coming into God's presence, in the way in which Habakkuk did, requires that we are 'teachable as well as frank', as David Prior puts it. We are to be submissive as well as honest, open to listening to what the Lord has to say to us.

He will change our lives if we come into his presence with this kind of submissive attitude. That was certainly the case for Habakkuk.

Sometimes we have the wrong attitude: we speak unwisely and act impulsively. Will you accept God's rebuke as a gracious display of his love for you? Will you submit to his discipline (Hebrews 12:5–6)?

Today, kneel in God's presence, bending your head and your heart humbly before him. Be like Mary, who sat at her Master's feet, listening and learning from him (Luke 10:38–42). Savour God's pleasure, knowing:

> These are the ones I look on with favour:
> > those who are humble and contrite in spirit,
> > and who tremble at my word.
>
> (Isaiah 66:2)

Day 9

Read Habakkuk 2:1–3
Key verse: Habakkuk 2:2

....

> [2] *Then the* LORD *replied:*
> *'Write down the revelation*
>   *and make it plain on tablets*
>   *so that a herald may run with it.'*

With our multiplicity of Bible versions and translations, we can become quite complacent about what we are actually reading.

Habakkuk 2:2 reminds us that we are holding God's Word in our hands. The key word in this exchange is 'revelation'. It is God's revealed Word that Habakkuk receives, and which he is told to write down so that the herald may run with it. And verse 2 points back to the opening verse of the prophecy, which describes the oracle that Habakkuk saw. It was this vision or revelation that God was calling him to record. The words of revelation from God are the vital turning point for Habakkuk, as they are for all of God's people who listen to his voice.

If we are perplexed about what is happening in the church, by the uncertainties of the world or the dilemmas in our own lives, then the starting point is to strengthen our confidence in God's revelation, his authoritative Word to us in all of the Scriptures. Men and women of faith believe that God's Word matters. That Word is authoritative, dynamic and life-giving. It is of lasting importance and must be preserved and passed on to others (2:2). As we come to the pages of Scripture, we look at that Word 'to see what he will say to me' (2:1). Throughout its pages, Scripture urges us to have responsive hearts.

John Calvin's commentary on this section of Habakkuk provides us with a lovely illustration:

> As long as we judge according to our own perceptions, we walk on the earth and while we do so, many clouds arise and Satan scatters ashes in our eyes and wholly darkens our judgment and thus it happens that we lie down altogether confounded. It is hence wholly necessary that we should tread our reason underfoot and come nigh to God himself. Let the word of God become our ladder. (Quoted in Elizabeth Achtemeier, *Nahum – Malachi: Interpretation*, John Knox Press, 1988, p. 41)

This very beautiful expression conveys exactly what Habakkuk did – coming humbly to God to receive his Word. This is our task as well: to let the Word of God become the ladder into God's presence, lifting us above the turmoil of this world so that we listen to God's will and purpose in Scripture and are determined to obey.

> If we forget that the newspapers are footnotes to Scripture and not the other way around, we will finally be afraid to get out of bed in the morning. The meaning of the world is most accurately given to us by God's Word.
>
> (Eugene Peterson, *Run with the Horses*, IVP, 1983, p. 54)
>
> Is there a situation in your personal life, church, community or the world where God's Word is challenging your thoughts and feelings? Will you allow Scripture to be your authority, the foundation of your confidence, the lens through which you understand the world?

Day 10

Read Habakkuk 2:1–5
Key verse: Habakkuk 2:3

....

> ³*For the revelation awaits an appointed time;*
> *it speaks of the end*
> *and will not prove false.*
> *Though it linger, wait for it;*
> *it will certainly come*
> *and will not delay.*

Are you known for keeping your promises?

Sometimes we worry when God doesn't act according to our timescale. However, verse 3 reminds us that there is an appointed time, a specific moment, when God's promise will be fulfilled. The ESV says, 'it hastens to the end': the verb conveys the sense of 'breathing' or 'panting', with the idea of gasping like a runner heading for the finishing line.

Habakkuk can be absolutely sure that what God now declares about the coming judgment of his people *will* take place. That is the first circle of application, the immediate context in which Habakkuk heard God's promise. And, sure enough, God's people were carried off into exile, just as Jeremiah had predicted. But the Babylonians, who were the tool in God's hand to bring about that initial judgment, would also be judged. God's Word had an appointed time for them as well. And we can go out in further concentric circles to the ultimate end, when God will finally act in judgment. Habakkuk is looking outwards and forwards to what the Old Testament calls the 'Day of the Lord' (see Joel 1:15; Amos 5:18), to what the New Testament refers to as the 'Day of Christ' (1 Corinthians 1:8; Philippians 1:6). There is an 'appointed time'. God speaks and God acts, whether in Habakkuk's day, our day or in that future day when everything will be put to rights through the coming of Christ.

If, like Habakkuk, we are tempted to think that God must have abandoned his people or given up on his promises, then we too must remember that 'the revelation awaits an appointed time'. I realize that this is rather cold comfort if you are going through difficulties. It doesn't always help for heartbroken people to be told to hang on, with the assurance that things will get better eventually. But from a pastoral point of view, it is very important to try to retain the longer-term perspective.

Hebrews 11 reminds us that Moses had this eternal perspective. He was 'looking ahead to his reward' (verse 26). The verb conveys the sense of fixing your eyes on something, like an artist intently gazing at the portrait she is painting. Faith that makes a difference is faith that fixes its eyes on the ultimate, not just the immediate. We must learn to take the long view, for God has today and tomorrow under his control.

A prime mark of the Christian mind is that it cultivates the eternal perspective. It looks beyond this life to another one. It is supernaturally orientated and brings to bear upon earthly considerations the fact of heaven and the fact of hell.

(Harry Blamires, *The Christian Mind*, SPCK, 1963)

Today, let 'the fact of heaven' guide your priorities, attitudes and behaviour.

Day 11

Read Habakkuk 2:1–5
Key verse: Habakkuk 2:3

....

> [3]*For the revelation awaits an appointed time;*
>   *it speaks of the end*
>   *and will not prove false.*
> *Though it linger, wait for it;*
>   *it will certainly come*
>   *and will not delay.*

Political spin and 'post truth' hit us from every angle. This constant stream of manipulation and deception washes over us daily.

In complete and refreshing contrast, God does not lie. And so it follows that because this revelation in chapter 2 is God speaking, 'It . . . will not prove false.' There is an absolute certainty about that word.

From where Habakkuk stood above Jerusalem on that day, appearances certainly seemed to contradict the message of God's ultimate control. In fact, the opposite seemed to be the case. Likewise for Abraham, who was told by God that he would be the father of many nations, appearances suggested the exact opposite, since not even a single child seemed possible. So the message to Habakkuk comes with this assurance: God is not stringing you along. He doesn't lie. 'It . . . will not prove false.'

Peter said exactly the same thing to the cynical people of his day. They doubted that the Lord would ever come back, that God would ever deliver on the promises he had made. And so Peter reminded them that when God spoke in creation, it produced results; when God spoke in judgment in Noah's day, no-one could avoid the resulting flood; and by that same word he will judge in the future (2 Peter 3:2–7). It is a reliable message: 'It . . . will not prove false.'

Isaiah uses the simple picture of the water cycle – the rain falls, achieves its purpose and then returns. He makes the connection: as in the natural world, so in the spiritual world. When God sends his word, it achieves its purpose. 'It . . . will accomplish what I desire and achieve the purpose for which I sent it' (Isaiah 55:11). Little by little, then, Habakkuk is learning that God is in control. It is a reliable message: 'It . . . will not prove false.'

Today, ask God to help you share his Word with others. Be alert for the opportunities he gives you. For example, you may have an opening to talk to a non-Christian friend about the reliability of Scripture. Perhaps you could text a verse of encouragement to a Christian friend going through difficult times, or you could read and talk about a Bible story with your children or grand-children. Remember:

The law of the LORD is perfect,
    refreshing the soul.
The statutes of the LORD are trustworthy,
    making wise the simple.
The precepts of the LORD are right,
    giving joy to the heart.
The commands of the LORD are radiant,
    giving light to the eyes.
The fear of the LORD is pure,
    enduring for ever.
The decrees of the LORD are firm,
    and all of them are righteous.
They are more precious than gold,
    than much pure gold;
they are sweeter than honey,
    than honey from the honeycomb.
(Psalm 19:7–10)

Day 12

Read Habakkuk 2:1–5
Key verses: Habakkuk 2:4–5

....

> ⁴*See, the enemy is puffed up;*
> *his desires are not upright –*
> *but the righteous person will live*
> *by his faithfulness –*
> ⁵*indeed, wine betrays him;*
> *he is arrogant and never at rest.*
> *Because he is as greedy as the grave*
> *and like death is never satisfied,*
> *he gathers to himself all the nations*
> *and takes captive all the peoples.*

We like having options. In fact, often we put off making decisions or plans, just in case a better option comes along.

But verse 4, the key verse of the whole book, confronts us with the reality that, ultimately, we have only two options: faith or unbelief.

> See, the enemy is puffed up;
>> his desires are not upright –
>> but the righteous person will live by his faithfulness.

This pithy statement sets the context for the whole book. It marks the contrast between the faithful righteous who trust God, and the proud, bloodthirsty Babylonians. It speaks of the contrasted motives of true and false living, of the godly and the ungodly, the Christian and the pagan perspective.

Habakkuk gives a graphic description of the ungodly. They are inflated with pride, completely self-reliant, and that, of course, is why they are unable to find a righteousness outside of themselves. They live their lives in a completely self-contained way, imagining that they need nothing. It is quite the opposite of Jesus' opening beatitude: 'How blest are those who know their need of God' (Matthew 5:3, NEB).

The ungodly delude themselves in their proud and arrogant independence. They are 'never at rest' – or as some translations say, 'he does not stay at home' (verse 5, NASB). They are restless with their consuming ambition to get more. Nothing will satisfy. Verse 5 explains that, like death itself, the ungodly person or nation just can't get enough. Here there is an echo of the description of the

Babylonians in chapter 1, swallowing up nations to satisfy their greedy appetite (verses 15–17).

Verses 4–5 give a sketch of the self-contained, self-obsessed person who shakes a little fist at God and says, 'I have no need of you.' Such a person is living a lie.

We are not immune from pride, arrogance and self-reliance. As Romans 6:11–14 teaches, we have to be intentional about saying 'no' to self. Helen Roseveare evokes a scene from her missionary days:

He [the African pastor] drew a straight line in the dirt floor with his heel. 'I,' he said, 'the capital I in our lives, Self, is the great enemy. Helen . . . the trouble with you is that we can see so much Helen that we cannot see Jesus. I notice that you drink much coffee. You stand there holding it, until it is cool enough to drink. May I suggest that as you stand and wait, you should just lift your heart to God and pray . . .' And as he spoke, he moved his heel in the dirt across the I he had previously drawn, 'Please, God, cross out the I.' There in the dirt was his lesson of simplified theology – the Cross – the crossed-out I life. 'I have been crucified with Christ and I no longer live, but Christ lives in me' (Galatians 2:20). (Noël Piper, *Faithful Women and Their Extraordinary God*, Crossway, 2005, p. 160)

Day 13

Read Habakkuk 2:1–5
Key verse: Habakkuk 2:4

....

> ⁴*See, the enemy is puffed up;*
> *his desires are not upright –*
> *but the righteous person will live*
> *by his faithfulness.*

What does it mean to 'live by faith'?

Habakkuk's phrase is actually used in several New Testament passages to express the heart of the Christian gospel. In Romans 1 Paul describes how all have sinned and deserve God's judgment. Justification is based not on what we do, but it is by faith in Jesus Christ alone, for Jew and Gentile alike. 'For in the gospel the righteousness of God is revealed – a righteousness that is by faith from first to last, just as it is written: "The righteous will live by faith"' (Romans 1:17).

Similarly, in Galatians 3 Paul asks how Abraham was made righteous. It was not through careful obedience to the law. No, a person is reckoned by God to be righteous on the basis of faith. We are justified freely by his grace. It is by faith in Christ's work on the cross that we are made right with God, and we can see how this attitude represents the exact opposite of the proud, self-sufficient unbeliever.

Habakkuk came to see that the attitude of steadfast faith is the only way to live. It is to recognize that the whole of your life is in God's hands. The writer to the Hebrews also quotes from Habakkuk 2:4, demonstrating that such faith is a matter of perseverance, waiting for what God has promised (Hebrews 10:36–39). The writer urges us to trust God that the Coming One will ultimately arrive.

> 'He who is coming will come
> and will not delay.'
> [Quoting Habakkuk 2:3, but changing 'it' to 'he'] . . .
> 'But my righteous one will live by faith.
> And I take no pleasure
> in the one who shrinks back.'
> But we do not belong to those who shrink back and are
> destroyed, but to those who have faith and are saved.

Faith involves not only the initial act of believing when we receive the gospel of God's grace, but also the steady perseverance of faithfulness. We depend entirely on him and we are to live day by day under the controlling principle that God is absolutely true to what he has said.

The word of the Lord to Habakkuk, and to all believers, is that the only way to live is by wholehearted trust in the God who rules the entire universe.

William McConnell was deputy governor of the Maze prison in Northern Ireland. Shortly before his assassination, he said,

> I have committed my life, talents, work and action to Almighty God, in the sure and certain knowledge that, however slight my hold of him may have been, his promises are sure and his hold on me complete.
> (Quoted by Roger Carswell, *Where Is God in a Messed-Up World?*, IVP, 2009, p. 131)

Do you share his conviction?

Will you live by faith, trusting God with your life, your family, your future and the world?

Day 14

Read Habakkuk 2:6–20
Key verses: Habakkuk 2:6–7

....

⁶Will not all of them taunt him with ridicule and scorn,
saying,
'Woe to him who piles up stolen goods
   and makes himself wealthy by extortion!
   How long must this go on?'
⁷Will not your creditors suddenly arise?
   Will they not wake up and make you tremble?
   Then you will become their prey.

For many people, shopping centres are the new places of worship. The creed of our day is grab all you can, look after number one. We are driven to want more and more, without regard for those we might injure in the process.

The Babylonians were also known for their greed and injustice. This taunt song (2:6–20) begins by mocking them for their selfish ambition. They robbed many nations and accumulated more and more by trampling on others.

They feathered their own nest at the expense of everybody else and constantly wanted more (see what Habakkuk said about the ungodly in chapter 2:5).

The outcome is described in verse 7. The proud Babylonians might think they are invincible; they might seem triumphant as they mock God, but they will not get away with it. Throughout this taunt song, we see that the Lord will turn the tables. The plunderer will be plundered (verse 8). The judgment of Babylon is recorded in Daniel chapter 5. Belshazzar, king of Babylon, was feasting, enjoying the fruit of all his ill-gotten gains, when the finger of God began writing on the wall: 'That very night Belshazzar, king of the Babylonians, was slain, and Darius the Mede took over the kingdom' (Daniel 5:30–31).

This is an important reminder for all who wonder about the apparent success of evil in our world, and might be tempted to imagine that the fat cats really will succeed. One day, God says, the plunderer will be plundered; the victor will become the victim.

Are you distressed at how evil is prospering in the world, in your community, in your office or college? Meditate on Psalm 73. The psalmist echoes Habakkuk's observation in chapter 2:4 that there are two ways to live: having faith in God or trusting your own rules (see also Matthew 7:13–14). He also reminds us that judgment is coming when God will right all wrongs. With this in mind, will you pray for increased desire and opportunity to share the gospel, even with those who appear to be prospering? Will you also pray that your resolve to live righteously would be strengthened?

> My flesh and my heart may fail,
> > but God is the strength of my heart
> > and my portion for ever.
> Those who are far from you will perish;
> > you destroy all who are unfaithful to you.
> But as for me, it is good to be near God.
> > I have made the Sovereign LORD my refuge;
> > I will tell of all your deeds.
> (Psalm 73:26–28)

Day 15

Read Habakkuk 2:6–20
Key verse: Habakkuk 2:9

· ·

> [9]*Woe to him who builds his house by unjust gain,*
>   *setting his nest on high*
>   *to escape the clutches of ruin!*

My wife and I recently enjoyed a friend's birthday party, but the conversations there surprised both of us. For Christian and non-Christian alike, the subject of security dominated the conversation. I suppose it was because most of us were fifty-somethings confronting our mid-life crises and wondering about the future!

Verse 9 is a graphic description of people or nations who think they are in control. In reality, it is a picture of false security. We know that one military manoeuvre employed by the Babylonians was to capture nations around them and thereby create buffer zones to provide a measure of security. Although the tactics are different, the attitude is common enough today. People do everything they can to protect themselves against disaster. Using whatever means at their disposal and with scant regard for the needs of others – not least, the poor and defenceless – they build their imagined security with wealth. They think they've made it, they've got away with it . . .

Or have they? In verse 11 the Lord again pronounces the outcome: the stones of their buildings will give testimony against them. Those who have built their fortresses on the basis of ill-gotten gain will discover that those very things will return to haunt them. Their schemes will backfire, and their great edifices will cry out for vengeance.

Nebuchadnezzar was enormously proud of his palace complex. In the outer courts the wall was some 136 feet (approx. 41 metres) thick, with each brick inscribed with the name 'Nebuchadnezzar'. And there is considerable irony in verse 10: 'You have forfeited your life.' Nebuchadnezzar of Babylon thought he had the whole world. But 'What good is it for someone to gain the whole world, yet forfeit their soul?' (Mark 8:36). It is a terrible thing to get to the end of your life and discover you have completely missed the point.

Maybe the graphic image of the stones of the wall crying out is a hint of what would happen when God's finger wrote the damning message on the walls of the king's palace. Once again, the message in Habakkuk's day and ours is plain. Judgment will come. The writing is on the wall. It is an inescapable certainty.

What 'buffer zones' have you created? What people and things provide you with a sense of security? Having spare cash in the bank, a pension plan, family living close by, a comfortable house? There is nothing intrinsically wrong with these things, but, if we are not careful, they lull us into a false sense of security. We trust them instead of trusting in God. Reflect on what it would mean for you to live with a true dependence on the security of Christ and his Word when we have so many material things that support us:

> Some trust in chariots and some in horses,
>   but we trust in the name of the Lord our God.
> (Psalm 20:7)

Day 16

Read Habakkuk 2:6–20
Key verses: Habakkuk 2:12–13

....

> [12] *Woe to him who builds a city with bloodshed*
> *and establishes a town by injustice!*
> [13] *Has not the LORD Almighty determined*
> *that the people's labour is only fuel for the fire,*
> *that the nations exhaust themselves for nothing?*

'People look at the outward appearance, but the LORD looks at the heart' (1 Samuel 16:7).

Nebuchadnezzar's palace would undoubtedly have impressed the tourists. The grand scale and magnificent opulence certainly drew the crowds, but it did not impress God. He saw something else. 'He saw only the blood of untold numbers of people who were slaughtered in ruthless warfare in order to obtain the means which made these buildings possible. He saw only the iniquity, the perversity, the crookedness of the builders' (Theo Latsch, quoted in R. D. Patterson, *Nahum, Habakkuk, Zephaniah: An Exegetical Commentary*, Moody Press, 1991, p. 194).

Despite Nebuchadnezzar's show of ruthless power, the outcome was devastating: it all goes up in smoke (see Jeremiah 51:58). The psalmist was absolutely right: 'Unless the LORD builds the house, the builders labour in vain' (Psalm 127:1). The word the psalmist uses for 'vain' is the same one used in verse 13: they are working for 'nothing'. It is the same message that was recorded by the Teacher in Ecclesiastes. Vanity! Futility! They are working for nothing more substantial than a puff of smoke.

The chapter makes it clear that everything the Babylonians have done will be fuel for the fire of God's judgment. And so it will be for all those who choose not the way of faith but the way of the proud. For the wicked, their world will be reduced to ashes; it will disappear in a cloud of smoke. How can we be certain? 'Has not the LORD Almighty determined' it? (verse 13). If he is the Lord Almighty, his judgment is certain and sure.

Judgment is certain because of the reality of God's holy character. Although sin inevitably produces its own destructive consequences, the book of Habakkuk reminds us that God's active judgment is also at work – if not immediately, then most certainly in the future. It is God's world and it is under his control. His judgment will surely punish sin and set things right.

Despite all the effort and attention to detail, Nebuchadnezzar's palace went up in a puff of smoke. This image takes us to 1 Corinthians 3, where Paul explains that our lives are secure on the one foundation of Jesus Christ, but he asks, what materials are you using as you build on that foundation? How you live your life now matters, because one day it will be tested. Will you look back on your life and see that you have built only with things that are temporary, or will you have used your time, gifts and talents to build something that will last for eternity? Will it disappear in a cloud of smoke because it has all been selfish ambition, or will it be lasting, built for eternity?

Day 17

Read Habakkuk 2:6–20
Key verses: Habakkuk 2:15–16

....

¹⁵*Woe to him who gives drink to his neighbours,*
pouring it from the wineskin till they are drunk,
so that he can gaze on their naked bodies!
¹⁶*You will be filled with shame instead of glory.*
Now it is your turn! Drink and let your nakedness
be exposed!
*The cup from the L*ORD*'s right hand is coming*
round to you,
and disgrace will cover your glory.

What lengths would you go to in order to get what you want?

Habakkuk lamented the Babylonians' shameless exploitation. They were damaging the environment and causing cruelty to animals (verse 17). They were also using alcohol to seduce people (verses 15–16). But the point of this woe is broader than that. The ungodly have very little respect for the dignity of other human beings. They will go to any means to achieve their purpose. Other people are simply objects to be manipulated and exploited. This appalling lack of regard for the dignity of others is the depraved behaviour of those who live their lives without God.

Notice the same pattern in this woe as in all the others. The wicked have brought shame on others, and so now the Lord will bring shame on them. We can imagine Belshazzar back at the feast. At the beginning of Daniel 5 they are in festive mood, for the Babylonians were renowned for their drunkenness. Then Belshazzar gave orders to bring in the gold and silver goblets that Nebuchadnezzar had taken from the temple in Jerusalem. And as they drank their wine and praised their gods, that very night the hand of the Sovereign Lord appeared and wrote on the wall. Habakkuk 2:16 was fulfilled: 'Now it is your turn! Drink . . . the cup from the LORD's right hand is coming round to you.'

Habakkuk chapter 2 reminds us that God sees what is happening and he acts. The cup of judgment will come. The image of the cup is used by various Old Testament prophets to express the same awful truth. 'This cup filled with the wine of my wrath,' records Jeremiah 25:15.

'A cup large and deep; it will bring scorn and derision,' predicts Ezekiel 23:32.

In fact, these words take us to Gethsemane. Jesus, who knew all of these Old Testament passages, takes from his Father the cup of judgment. It is no wonder that initially he shrank from taking it, for the cup represented God's judgment, which our sins deserved, but which Jesus was to face at the cross. He drank that cup to the dregs: he bore our sin and took our judgment.

Jesus' drinking of that cup of judgment means that we will never hear God's 'woe' to us. For all true believers, Paul's confident assertion should be written across the woes of Habakkuk chapter 2: 'There is now no condemnation for those who are in Christ Jesus' (Romans 8:1). Today, praise God for this gospel truth and determine to live in the light of it.

Day 18

Read Habakkuk 2:6–20
Key verses: Habakkuk 2:18–19

∙∙

¹⁸Of what value is an idol carved by a craftsman?
  Or an image that teaches lies?
For the one who makes it trusts in his own creation;
  he makes idols that cannot speak.
¹⁹Woe to him who says to wood, 'Come to life!'
  Or to lifeless stone, 'Wake up!'
Can it give guidance?
  It is covered with gold and silver;
  there is no breath in it.

It has been well said that when people stop believing in truth, they don't believe in nothing; they believe in anything.

Here the woe is the folly of worshipping dumb idols. The Babylonians often ascribed their success to their gods and looked for guidance from idols of their own making. There is a fair amount of satirical mockery in verses 18 and 19, as in descriptions of idolatry elsewhere in the Old Testament, and the purpose is to demonstrate the difference between the powerless non-entities of the pagan nations and Israel's living, all-powerful, all-controlling God:

> For the one who makes it trusts in his own creations;
>> he makes idols that cannot speak . . .
> Can it give guidance?'
> (verses 18–19)

We may think this is merely pagan religion, distant from contemporary Western culture, but it is very typical of our society as well. People long for guidance, hoping to make sense of their lives and gain some control. So they turn to astrology, Ouija boards or New Age superstitions. Contemporary idolatry is all around us. Every generation seeks substitute deities. Perhaps most obviously in our culture, the main idol is the self. The social commentator Bryan Appleyard suggests,

> The only possible sin today is the sin against oneself. The idea is everywhere – self-help, self-esteem, making the best of oneself, looking one's best and self-realisation are the great contemporary virtues. Therefore the one recognised sin is failure to look after *numero uno*.
> (Bryan Appleyard, 'Are You Sinning Comfortably?', *The Times*, 11 April 2004)

We have become the centre of our own little universe. And whatever the substitute god might be – possessions, plans or self-obsession – God pronounces his woe upon all who trust in the things of their own creation. Notice verse 18: 'Of what value is an idol carved by a craftsman? Or an image that teaches lies?' It's an intriguing suggestion – an idol that lies. It is counterfeit. The idols in people's lives are self-deceiving, blinding them to their own help-lessness. The supposed worship of an idol blinds them about their guilt and their need of forgiveness. They are ignorant of the fact that they depend on God himself for every breath they take.

Many idols vie to displace God from his rightful place on the throne of your life. How is your obsession with 'self' diminishing your devotion to God? None of us is immune. Even John the Baptist acknowledged, 'He must become greater; I must become less' (John 3:30). Ask God for strength and wisdom to tackle this idol.

Have Thine own way, Lord! Have Thine own way!
Thou art the Potter, I am the clay.
Mould me and make me after Thy will,
While I am waiting, yielded and still.

Have Thine own way, Lord! Have Thine own way!
Hold o'er my being absolute sway!
Fill with Thy Spirit till all shall see
Christ only, always, living in me.
(Adelaide Pollard, 1907)

Day 19

Read Habakkuk 2:6–20
Key verse: Habakkuk 2:20

....

> ²⁰*The Lord is in his holy temple;*
>   *let all the earth be silent before him.*

When life does not turn out as we'd anticipated, we have a certainty we can cling to: 'The Lord is in his holy temple, let all the earth be silent before him' (verse 20).

This verse comes in the middle of the sequence of woes where the idols are declared to be dumb – silent. Unlike the idols, God is never unable to hear, speak or act. He is the Lord of heaven and earth. The word 'silent' is onomatopoeic in Hebrew, like our word 'hush': be silent, stop all the arguments, all the arrogant assertions of human power, the efforts of human glory, the petty ambitions. It is a call for reverence, because the one who is speaking is the Lord of the universe. He is the Sovereign Lord, active in history; he calls all men and women, all nations and governments, to bow the knee to him.

In these few words we have the answer to Habakkuk's complaint. Why isn't God acting in the way Habakkuk thought he should? The answer is stated in a simple assertion. The Lord is seated on his kingly throne, in the place of ultimate authority, above heaven and earth, high above his creatures. Before him there is no room for asserting our independence. Instead, we are called to humble submission to the Lord of the universe. Unlike the impotent deities of paganism, here is the God who is in control, who can be relied upon. Here is absolute certainty, for this God is the unchanging Ruler of the universe, which he created and sustains and which ultimately he will wrap up and bring to completion. The people in Habakkuk's day were foolish to turn to the substitute 'godlets', whether idols, magic or black arts, for they were called into relationship with the Sovereign Lord.

The simplicity of verse 20 speaks clearly to the fractured world of our day too. The more we grow in our understanding of the majesty of the God whom we worship – the God who calls us into fellowship with himself and who cares for his children – the more we will learn to entrust the uncertainties of our lives to his good purposes.

Lift the curtain of heaven and glimpse the Lord on his throne. Read Isaiah 6, Ezekiel 1, Daniel 7 or Revelation 4, and imagine the scene those writers saw: 'I saw the Lord, high and exalted, seated on a throne; and the train of his robe filled the temple' (Isaiah 6:1). Whatever problems or issues you are facing today – anxiety about the future, ill health, unanswered prayers, financial struggles or family strife – remember this certainty: 'The Lord is in his holy temple.' Repeat this phrase as you bring your prayer requests to God. Our sovereign God is on the throne. He is in complete control over all the various strands of our lives and he will fulfil his good purposes in and through you.

Day 20

Read Habakkuk 2:6–20
Key verse: Habakkuk 2:14

• •

> ¹⁴*For the earth will be filled with the knowledge*
> *of the glory of the Lord*
> *as the waters cover the sea.*

In a pitch-black room, even the faintest flicker of a candle makes all the difference. And verse 14 is an incredible shaft of light in the darkness of Habakkuk's prophecy.

Here, in the context of the power of empires and the pretensions of human rulers, the Lord speaks of the certainty of what will be left on that final day: the universal knowledge of the glory of God. Similar words are used by Isaiah:

> They will neither harm nor destroy
>   on all my holy mountain,
> for the earth will be full of the knowledge of the Lord
>   as the waters cover the sea.
> (Isaiah 11:9)

The earlier part of Isaiah 11 refers to a shoot that will come up from the stump of Jesse. It is a prophecy of great David's Greater Son, pointing towards the ultimate victory of the Lord Jesus, to the completion of his purposes in the destruction of evil and the establishment of a new heaven and earth, the home of righteousness.

Intriguingly, Habakkuk adds to the words of Isaiah; he includes the word 'glory'. 'The earth will be filled with the knowledge of the *glory* of the Lord.' Why is that? Perhaps because the word 'glory' encompasses the ultimate goal of all human history. If we are uncertain about what is happening in our world, we should remember that this is where everything is heading. The ultimate truth, the final word, the enduring reality, will be the glory of the Lord. And all other human glories, such as those described and mocked in the woes of chapter 2, will fade away in the light of that supreme glory, his royal majesty. It is a wonderful description of the ultimate triumph of God.

The last word will not belong to earth's kingdoms. Habakkuk gives us a very different perspective of who is in control. It will be a glorious world with the awareness of God's purposes, presence and glory.

What are you passionate about? What puts a smile on your face, gets your heart racing and causes you willingly to make sacrifices?

God's passion is for his own glory. He is jealous that his name be treasured and magnified above all else, and he wants this to be your chief passion too. What would that look like? It will mean a readiness to 'declare his glory among the nations' – sharing the good news of the gospel with friends, neighbours, work colleagues, calling them to worship him (Psalm 96:3). It will also mean being intentional about your inner life: rooting out idols, those relationships and things that compete for first place in your heart. The goal is to make God your all-consuming treasure.

As John Piper says, 'God is most glorified in us when we are most satisfied in him' (*Desiring God*, IVP, 2004, p. 10).

Day 21

Read Habakkuk 3:1–2
Key verse: Habakkuk 3:2

....

2 *LORD, I have heard of your fame;*
  I stand in awe of your deeds, LORD.
Repeat them in our day,
  in our time make them known;
  in wrath remember mercy.

Do you enjoy singing?

You don't need to have the most melodious voice or be able to read music to sing. In fact, singing about what God has done for you is one of the best ways to help you persevere during difficult days. Just think about Paul and Silas in their prison cell (Acts 16)!

Although it is introduced as a prayer, there are several clues that chapter 3 is actually a song. *Selah* (verses 3, 9, 13) is a term possibly designating a musical break; at the close of the chapter there is a musical instruction (verse 19); and in verse 1 there is a rather unusual word, *shigionoth*, probably an instruction about tempo which implies a strong rhythm. This particular song was no funeral dirge. Given its extraordinarily dramatic descriptions and dynamic pace, it was certainly up-tempo. As we read it, we can almost hear the brass section, the drums, the driving rhythm of the bass! So after all we have looked at, all of the struggles, challenges and turmoil that Habakkuk had faced, what does he do? He starts to sing – and he encourages others to start singing too.

> LORD, I have heard of your fame;
>> I stand in awe of your deeds, LORD.
> (verse 2)

We can sense immediately the change of tone from the anxious prayers and appeals of chapter 1. Here there is a sense of humble commitment. Habakkuk is no longer arguing, for he recognizes that everything that God has said and done is just. Calvin translates the verse: 'I heard Thy voice.' Standing there on the walls above Jerusalem, Habakkuk had heard God's word, the report of God's work, both in the past and in the prophecies of what was to come. He stands in awe, probably alarmed, with a sense of submission and godly fear.

We will see this stated even more starkly when we come to verse 16. But by this point in the prophecy, Habakkuk has recognized that God is in control of the situation. He is ready to accept God's just purposes. It is a kind of 'Amen' to what God had been saying to him, a humble response: 'Yes, Lord, now I understand. It is your work.'

Today, will you sing to God? Not because your circumstances are wonderful, but because you acknowledge his control, you accept his purposes and you want him to continue his work.

Because you are my help,
    I sing in the shadow of your wings.
(Psalm 63:7)

I will sing of the LORD's great love for ever;
    with my mouth I will make your faithfulness known
    through all generations.
I will declare that your love stands firm for ever,
    that you have established your faithfulness in
        heaven itself.
(Psalm 89:1–2)

I will sing of your love and justice;
    to you, LORD, I will sing praise.
(Psalm 101:1)

Day 22

Read Habakkuk 3:1–2
Key verse: Habakkuk 3:2

....

> ²*L*ORD*, I have heard of your fame;*
> *I stand in awe of your deeds, L*ORD*.*
> *Repeat them in our day,*
> *in our time make them known;*
> *in wrath remember mercy.*

What are you praying for?

Habakkuk prays fervently that God's powerful work in the past would be seen in his own day, so that the people of God would know that he is in control of their lives and of history (verse 2). Chapter 3 has many references to the story of the exodus, celebrated frequently by the psalmists and the prophets as their finest hour. And so he appeals, 'Please, Lord, repeat that kind of redemption. Renew your work now and act just as you did in the past.' It is a call for God's action. He wants to see the work of God in the past renewed now, not in the distant future. And he is clear about what matters: renew *your* work. He wants God's purposes fulfilled, God's work established in his day. It is a prayer with which we are familiar: 'Your kingdom come, your will be done.'

As I read these verses, I can't help thinking about what dominates my praying. Is this the kind of prayer that I pray? Am I longing for God's purposes to be fulfilled, for the church to be renewed? Christians in Europe live in a continent where, by and large, the church is not growing. The majority of God's people today are found in the southern hemisphere, and one reason for this shift in the centre of gravity is undoubtedly the extraordinary gospel passion and committed prayer of Christians in these countries. I have a friend who lives and works in the Majority World, and he wonders if there is some relation between the suffering, poverty and daily challenge of living in some of these countries and the extraordinary sense of dependence that Christians express – and therefore the blessing of God that they enjoy. There is surely a correlation between those things: dependent prayer and God's blessing.

When Habakkuk appeals, 'in our day, in our time', perhaps he means 'Even in the midst of judgment, Lord, come in deliverance.' Habakkuk does not want an experience that is just hearsay or second-hand. Rather, he appeals that they would experience God's saving presence now, just as they did in the past.

We want God to act in our day, but for some reason that is not reflected in our prayer life. If we are honest, most of our prayers tend to stay close to home, concerned with the needs of family and friends. Today, will you start to pray like Habakkuk? Will you look up, look out, and plead with God to act in your day and generation?

Oh, that you would rend the heavens and come down,
    that the mountains would tremble before you!
As when fire sets twigs ablaze
    and causes water to boil,
come down to make your name known to your
        enemies
    and cause the nations to quake before you!
(Isaiah 64:1–2)

Day 23

Read Habakkuk 3:1–2
Key verse: Habakkuk 3:2

....

> *2LORD, I have heard of your fame;*
> *I stand in awe of your deeds, LORD.*
> *Repeat them in our day,*
> *in our time make them known;*
> *in wrath remember mercy.*

I saw a cartoon not long ago, depicting a husband and wife standing in a queue before the gates of heaven. Waiting for their turn to face judgment, the wife whispered to her husband, 'Now, Harold, whatever you do, please don't demand what's coming to you.'

Despite being aware of what our rebellion deserves, we are still uncomfortable with the idea of God's wrath. Some Christians today hesitate to ascribe such emotions to God. We might be disturbed to discover that, in the Old Testament alone, there are over twenty words for God's wrath and anger, and apparently over 580 references to him acting in that way.

Indeed, wrath is essential to our understanding of God. How can God be God if he does not reveal his wrath 'against all the godlessness and wickedness of people' (Romans 1:18)? Paradoxically, it is because of God's wrath against wickedness that we have the comfort of knowing that his justice will be fulfilled, that the day of restoration will finally come.

Nevertheless, we can identify with Habakkuk's cry: 'in wrath remember mercy.' He had heard of God's judgment on his own people in Judah, the fearful reality of God's anger against sin, and so he prays that, alongside God's wrath, he would remember mercy. Once again, his prayer is a model to us. The essence of prayer is to plead God's character in God's presence. Remember mercy, Lord. Be true to your character.

It is important to hold these two truths of mercy and wrath together, for sometimes Christians tend to emphasize one truth over another. In our desire to make the Christian message acceptable, we might be tempted to emphasize God's love and play down the idea of his wrath. But the Bible frequently describes this duality within God. God's wrath and mercy belong together as two dynamic concepts, which are complementary both in God's nature and in his actions.

In our praying, we must take the words of Habakkuk's prayer and appeal to God's mercy on the grounds of Christ's work. Whatever Habakkuk teaches us about the inevitability of judgment and God's wrath, it also points us to the Lord who shows mercy.

Confess your personal sins and the sins of our nation to God. Cry out to him, 'In wrath remember mercy.'

Pray with King David:

> Have mercy on me, O God,
>   according to your unfailing love;
> according to your great compassion
>   blot out my transgressions.
> Wash away all my iniquity
>   and cleanse me from my sin.
> For I know my transgressions,
>   and my sin is always before me.
> Against you, you only, have I sinned
>   and done what is evil in your sight;
> so you are right in your verdict
>   and justified when you judge.
> (Psalm 51:1–4)

Day 24

Read Habakkuk 3:3–15
Key verses: Habakkuk 3:3–4

•••

> ³*God came from Teman,*
> *the Holy One from Mount Paran.*
> *His glory covered the heavens*
> *and his praise filled the earth.*
> ⁴*His splendour was like the sunrise;*
> *rays flashed from his hand,*
> *where his power was hidden.*

What will it be like when the Lord returns?

Eugene Peterson describes it like this:

> Skies are blazing with his splendor,
> his praises sounding through the earth.
> His cloud-brightness like dawn, exploding, spreading,
> forked-lightning shooting from his hand –
> what power hidden in that fist!
> (Habakkuk 3:4, MSG)

This vision, which swept Habakkuk off his feet (see 3:2, 16), begins by proclaiming that God is on the move. As he draws nearer, the impact of his glorious presence becomes more and more dramatic. Verse 3 is a reference to the area of Sinai where God first revealed himself to Moses at the burning bush and where, subsequently, in a dramatic revelation of his power and presence, he revealed the law to his people.

Verses 3 and 4 conjure up the images of fire and cloud that characterized that Mount Sinai encounter, reminding Habakkuk and all singers of this song of the glory and power of God whenever he comes to his people. Just as at Sinai, his coming is accompanied by a radiance that is overwhelming and awe-inspiring. Habakkuk sees it here illuminating the entire world.

He remembers those great events of the past, but, as throughout the song, there is also an anticipation of God's future intervention. His coming will always be a source of hope for God's people. As we saw earlier, the writer to the Hebrews quotes from Habakkuk chapter 2:3, making application to the coming of the Lord: 'Do not throw away your confidence; it will be richly rewarded. You need to persevere . . . For, in just a very little while, "He who is coming will come and will not delay"' (Hebrews 10:35–37). The glorious manifestation of God's coming described in

Habakkuk 3:3–4, witnessed by the entire universe, also anticipates that day when we will see Jesus coming (see also Matthew 24:27, 30).

Habakkuk's vision is pointing us to that ultimate day. In essence, God is saying, 'Watch, I am coming.' It will be a day of judgment and of deliverance, a day of wrath and of mercy, a day when human history will finally be wrapped up. We are to look 'for the blessed hope – the appearing of the glory of our great God and Saviour, Jesus Christ' (Titus 2:13).

Habakkuk does not receive a neat solution to his problems. Instead, he is given an overwhelming vision of the coming of the Lord. Today, meditate on John's vision of Christ's return in Revelation 1:12–18. One day soon he 'will come down from heaven, with a loud command, with the voice of the archangel and with the trumpet call of God' (1 Thessalonians 4:16). Jesus will be 'revealed from heaven in blazing fire with his powerful angels' (2 Thessalonians 1:7), 'every eye will see him' (Revelation 1:7), and 'every knee will bow' (Romans 14:11).

Keep this vision in the forefront of your mind today. It won't change your situation, but it will help you persevere and focus on what really matters.

Day 25

Read Habakkuk 3:3–15
Key verses: Habakkuk 3:6–7

....

⁶He stood, and shook the earth;
he looked, and made the nations tremble.
The ancient mountains crumbled
and the age-old hills collapsed –
but he marches on for ever.
⁷I saw the tents of Cushan in distress,
the dwellings of Midian in anguish.

We like to feel in control. It gives us a sense of comfort, security and, at times, power.

Habakkuk stops us in our tracks and reminds us that God is the one who is all-powerful. He is in control.

Just as there were great convulsions at Sinai when God came to his people, so his power is demonstrated whenever he comes in salvation and deliverance. The poetry of verse 6 demonstrates the almost cosmic implications of his arrival. He is the Creator, and at his coming even the mountains crumble before him. The eternal hills bow before the splendour of this eternal God. Cushan and Midian were nations that bordered Egypt, so they would have seen the great deliverance that God brought about for his people and would have trembled with distress and anguish (verse 7). In Habakkuk's vision no nation will be exempt from his power and his judgment.

Many of the descriptive images in Habakkuk 3 are picked up in the New Testament. Peter describes the cataclysmic events of the end times:

> The heavens will disappear with a roar; the elements will be destroyed by fire, and the earth and everything done in it will be laid bare . . . That day will bring about the destruction of the heavens by fire, and the elements will melt in the heat. But in keeping with his promise we are looking forward to a new heaven and a new earth, where righteousness dwells.
>
> (2 Peter 3:10, 12–13)

Peter is making it abundantly clear to the people of his day, just as Habakkuk did, that this *will* happen. God is in control of this world. As Habakkuk says at the end of verse 6, 'His ways are eternal' (AMP). We are reminded once again: he is in control.

In chapter 3 Habakkuk is describing the powerful Lord of the universe, the one who is eternal. He is the Sovereign Lord, in control of creation, history and all of the nations. No wonder they will tremble at his coming! The power of the Lord is the foundation for our security and comfort in hard-pressed situations.

It only takes the result of a blood test, a freak accident or unexpected news for our world to turn upside down. We soon realize that we have very little control over the circumstances of our lives. Thank God that when we are powerless, he is all-powerful. When our lives seem to spin out of control, he remains sovereign. The truth is that when we trust in what Christ achieved for us on the cross, we are eternally secure. So, whatever happens in life, we can be confident of God's eternal control, and that is the basis for our perseverance, joy and hope. Today, praise God that he has set your feet on a rock and given you a firm place to stand (Psalm 40:2).

Day 26

Read Habakkuk 3:8–15
Key verses: Habakkuk 3:12–13

....

> ¹² *In wrath you strode through the earth*
>   *and in anger you threshed the nations.*
> ¹³ *You came out to deliver your people,*
>   *to save your anointed one.*
> *You crushed the leader of the land of wickedness,*
>   *you stripped him from head to foot.*

Do you remember Habakkuk's first prayer: 'How long . . . must I cry for help, but you do not listen?' (1:2). Chapter 3 is the proof that God hears and acts, for this is an account of God's deliverance of his people. It was the very thing that Habakkuk was crying out for, the assurance he needed that God keeps his promises and remembers his covenant.

The poetry is powerful. God tramples the enemy under his feet and crushes the head of the wicked. With allusions to the Red Sea deliverance, God is portrayed as the general leading his forces to victory. And the battle is fought for one clear purpose. Although there are descriptions of judgment, there are also significant references to salvation. Notice in verse 8 that God is riding upon his chariot to victory. The word used for 'victory' is actually 'salvation'. The Greek version of the Old Testament renders it: 'Your chariot which is salvation'.

The purpose of God's coming is the salvation of his people (verse 13). What God did in the exodus deliverance he will do again. He will rescue his people and bring them home. That was fulfilled for some of God's people after the immediate judgment that Habakkuk and Jeremiah had predicted, for after the exile some finally returned to Jerusalem. But these verses also anticipate the deliverance of God's people in the future. Verse 13 speaks about 'your anointed one'. The anointed one is the Messiah, translated in the Greek as 'Christ'. The word 'anointed' was sometimes used of the kings of Israel, even of a pagan king, Cyrus, who was used by God to deliver his people. But the word also points to the true Messiah, Jesus, the Christ. At the cross, the Lord Jesus was our substitute in bearing God's righteous anger. It was there that wrath and mercy met. God raised Jesus to life – or to use the language of verse 13 – 'saved his anointed'. So Jesus won the decisive battle over human sin, over all of the cosmic hosts of wickedness. What Habakkuk described in his overwhelming vision was finally fulfilled in Christ: the victory of the Lord.

Perhaps Paul had Habakkuk's vision in mind when he described Christ's work on the cross: 'Having disarmed the powers and authorities, he made a public spectacle of them, triumphing over them by the cross' (Colossians 2:15). Today you will feel the pull of sin and witness the influence of evil, but Christ's death and resurrection mean his victory is certain. So:

- You don't need to fear evil.
- You don't need to give in to sin.
- You don't need to be riddled with guilt because of past sins.
- You are free to serve Christ.

Day 27

Read Habakkuk 3:16–19
Key verse: Habakkuk 3:16

....

¹⁶*I heard and my heart pounded,*
   my lips quivered at the sound;
decay crept into my bones,
   and my legs trembled.
Yet I will wait patiently for the day of calamity
   to come on the nation invading us.

Habakkuk had got the message.

Having encountered God's majesty and power, having seen God's judgment, he was shaken to the core of his being. His response is described either side of the vision, in verses 2 and 16, which are both saying similar things. He trembled like a leaf; he shook from head to toe; he was speechless. Habakkuk records that he felt the impact of this encounter, not simply hearing God's word, but now experiencing God himself. In the past he had questioned God about his character, his work and his righteousness. He had appealed for evidence of God's power and control in this uncertain world of his. And now that he had heard, now that he had seen the vision, the revelation from the Lord, he could barely stand up. He was profoundly shaken with a sense of awe, a deep respect for the Lord.

Habakkuk's reaction wasn't simply fear as he thought about the judgment to come, though doubtless that contributed to it. His reaction must also have been a response to the extraordinary revelation of God's character that he had just experienced in the vision of chapter 3.

There are many examples in the Bible of a similar reaction on the part of those who came into God's presence. Job's response to his encounter with the living God was 'I am unworthy' (Job 40:4). Like Habakkuk, he was speechless in the face of what God had said and done. Was Isaiah proud that he had been enabled to witness the greatness and holiness of God? Quite the reverse. He cried out, 'Woe to me! . . . I am ruined! For I am a man of unclean lips' (Isaiah 6:5).

Every so often in the Gospels there are glimpses of Jesus' own glory and power. Following that incredible fishing expedition, Peter finally said, 'Go away from me, Lord; I am a sinful man!' (Luke 5:8). And what was John's response when he had a profound vision of the ascended Christ amongst the lampstands? 'When I saw him, I fell at his feet as though dead' (Revelation 1:17).

Today, enter God's presence with reverence and awe.

> Unaccustomed as we are to mystery, we expect nothing even similar to Abraham's falling on his face, Moses' hiding in terror, Isaiah's crying out 'Woe is me', or Saul being knocked flat . . . Reverence and awe have often been replaced by a yawn of familiarity. The consuming fire has been domesticated into a candle flame, adding a bit of religious atmosphere, perhaps but no heat, no blinding light, no power for purification . . . We prefer the illusion of a safer deity and so we have pared God down to manageable proportions.
>
> (Donald McCullough, *The Trivialization of God*, cited in Peter Lewis, *The Message of the Living God*, IVP, 2000, pp. 320–321)

Silence the grumbling and the questions. Get rid of over familiarity. Take a step back and gaze at the majestic holiness of Almighty God. Get on your knees and worship him.

Day 28

Read Habakkuk 3:16–19
Key verse: Habakkuk 3:16

••

> ¹⁶*I heard and my heart pounded,*
> *my lips quivered at the sound;*
> *decay crept into my bones,*
> *and my legs trembled.*
> *Yet I will wait patiently for the day of calamity*
> *to come on the nation invading us.*

Habakkuk declares, 'I will wait patiently.'

The situation hasn't changed. 'Nations still rage . . . the arrogant still rule, the poor still suffer; the enslaved still labour for emptiness and false gods are still worshipped' (Elizabeth Achtemeier, *Nahum – Malachi: Interpretation*, John Knox Press, 1986, p. 58). But Habakkuk knows the one who is working out his purposes, unseen behind the turmoil. Habakkuk knows the end. He knows that God's Word can be trusted and his promises will be fulfilled (2:3).

Habakkuk shows us how to live in the meantime, how to live in the waiting room. Not with anxiety, not with uncertainty, but resting in the sure knowledge that the God who has spoken will bring about his purposes, that the earth will be filled with the knowledge of the glory of God. 'The righteous shall live by his faith' (Habakkuk 2:4, ESV). The Lord had told Habakkuk in chapter 2 to take the long-run perspective. And the patient waiting here in 3:16 is part of that same response.

How was he able to rest, to wait patiently? It was his faith in the word of God, that word of revelation. There would be discipline for God's people – he knew that was coming. Both he and Jeremiah had prophesied it and, as promised, the people were carted off into exile by the Babylonians (1:6). And now, at the close of his prophecy, Habakkuk points to the inevitable judgment on their enemies too (3:16). Sure enough, Nebuchadnezzar, Belshazzar and all subsequent empires have been judged by God.

Habakkuk had to look through the fog as he wondered about God's purposes and whether God really was in control. But, as believers in Jesus Christ, we now know what God's ultimate purposes are. They are expressed in Paul's incredible mission statement in Ephesians. He tells us that God will 'bring unity to all things in heaven and on earth under Christ' (Ephesians 1:10). So the Christian church must also walk by faith. We too must rest in God's promise and trust in his Word as we wait for that final deliverance.

The Victorian pastor and preacher Charles Spurgeon said,

> We have been assured by people who think they know a great deal about the future that awful times are coming. Be it so; it need not alarm us, for the Lord reigneth. Stay yourself on the Lord . . . and you can rejoice in His name. If the worst comes to the worst, our refuge is in God; if the heavens shall fall, the God of heaven will stand; when God cannot take care of His people under heaven, He will take them above the heavens and there they shall dwell with Him. Therefore, as far as you are concerned, rest; for you shall stand . . . at the end of the days.
>
> (Quoted in Elizabeth Achtemeier, *Nahum – Malachi*, p. 60)

Day 29

Read Habakkuk 3:16–19
Key verses: Habakkuk 3:17–18

....

¹⁷*Though the fig-tree does not bud*
and there are no grapes on the vines,
though the olive crop fails
and the fields produce no food,
though there are no sheep in the sheepfold
and no cattle in the stalls,
¹⁸*yet I will rejoice in the LORD,*
I will be joyful in God my Saviour.

Everything had gone.

It is possible that Habakkuk is anticipating the ultimate Day of the Lord. But it is also highly likely that he is describing the devastating impact of the predicted invasion of the Babylonians described in chapter 1. Verse 17 begins with the apparent luxuries of figs, grapes and olives, but moves very quickly to show that there is no food at all. It wasn't simply a devastated economic and social infrastructure, but total destruction.

That's what makes this small word 'yet' all the more remarkable. Habakkuk is stripped of everything and still this man of faith sings, 'Yet I will rejoice in the LORD' (verse 18). It is Job saying, 'Though he slay me, yet I will hope in him' (Job 13:15). It is Paul saying, 'We are hard pressed on every side, but not crushed' (2 Corinthians 4:8).

How can Habakkuk respond as he does? What was there left for him to rejoice in? It was not his possessions; it was certainly not his circumstances. Like Job, he was stripped of everything else but God. And that is the key to his joy; it is finding that God the Creator, the Redeemer, the covenant-keeping God is enough. That is how Habakkuk concludes his prophecy. All of those things on which we rely may be stripped away, but God is enough.

All we have seen in the book of Habakkuk points us to this fact: for men and women of faith, evil has lost the initiative. When we become Christians, we are not protected from the hardships of this world. There is no guarantee that we will be immune from suffering or from God's discipline, from the oppression of enemies, or from the pains and dangers of living in this broken world. But we know that the Lord will not let go of his people, that he has not abandoned his world. He is still in control and his purposes will be fulfilled.

People of faith have discovered that Habakkuk's song rings true. When everything is taken away, we can say, 'I will rejoice in God.'

As you face life's uncertainties and turbulence, will you respond like Habakkuk: 'Yet I will rejoice in the LORD, I will be joyful in God my Saviour'? When everything you have come to rely on is stripped away, will you acknowledge that God is enough?

Meditate on Paul's words. What do they mean for you today?

Who shall separate us from the love of Christ? Shall trouble or hardship or persecution or famine or nakedess or danger or sword? . . . No . . . I am convinced that neither death nor life, neither angels nor demons, neither the present nor the future, nor any powers, neither height nor depth, nor anything else in all creation, will be able to separate us from the love of God that is in Christ Jesus our Lord.
(Romans 8:35, 37–39)

Day 30

Read Habakkuk 3:16–19
Key verse: Habakkuk 3:19

....

> ¹⁹ *The Sovereign L*ORD *is my strength;*
>   *he makes my feet like the feet of a deer,*
>   *he enables me to tread on the heights.*

Many of us experience 'spiritual vertigo'. We grow queasy at the thought of some of the spiritual challenges, the mountains, which lie ahead of us. Our legs begin to buckle when we think about threatening circumstances. So the result is that we live our lives within cautiously safe limits.

Because of his encounter with the living God, Habakkuk knew he could face these spiritual challenges. He declared, 'The LORD is my strength.' The Hebrew word could also mean 'army'. The Lord is my army, the one who sustains my life, the life of the 'righteous who live by faith'. He provides for the person who might have lost everything else and been pushed right to the limits. He is all I need.

This is similar to Paul's testimony in 2 Corinthians 12. Frequently, Paul had prayed for the removal of his thorn in the flesh. And how did the Lord reply? 'My grace is sufficient for you, for my power is made perfect in weakness' (verse 9). It was an unexpected answer, but it made a powerful impact on Paul's life. Now God's all-sufficient grace was poured into his life, not in spite of the thorn but because of that very weakness. The breakthrough for Paul was to see that weakness has the special advantage of making room for God's grace. It is when God can work most effectively, when his power can be seen most clearly.

As with Paul, God was giving Habakkuk a strength that would enable him to accept his weakness and fears and still stand up to the world. He is now sure-footed. He has both stability and energy: 'He enables me to tread on the heights' (verse 19). So, as I put my faith in him, I can live with unstumbling security, rising above all of the oppression of the world. God enables his people to keep walking, to keep climbing.

Some writers remind us that 'the heights' could refer to the 'high places', those centres of pagan worship. It was thought that the gods controlled the high ground and were therefore in charge of the whole area. So is it possible that Habakkuk means that God enables us to go even into those spiritual territories, those high places of the enemy? By God's power, by God's Word and by God's Spirit, he enables us to see the gospel advance, whatever the situation, whatever hostile forces may be ranged against Christ and against his people. He enables me to go on to those very heights.

Are you looking up at an impossibly high mountain, wondering how you are going to face this next spiritual challenge? Meditate on Psalm 121. Lean on the Lord's strength. He will enable you and keep your feet from slipping:

> I lift up my eyes to the mountains –
> where does my help come from?
> My help comes from the Lord,
> the Maker of heaven and earth.
> He will not let your foot slip –
> he who watches over you will not slumber.
> (Psalm 121:1–3)

For further study

If you would like to do further study on Habakkuk, the following books may be useful:

- David W. Baker, *Nahum, Habakkuk, Zephaniah*, Tyndale Old Testament Commentary (IVP, 2009)

- James Bruckner, *Jonah, Nahum, Habakkuk, Zephaniah*, NIV Application Commentary (Zondervan, 2004)

- John Mackay, *God's Just Demands: Jonah, Micah, Nahum, Habakkuk, Zephaniah* (Christian Focus, 2008)

- O. Palmer Robertson, *The Books of Nahum, Habakkuk and Zephaniah*, New International Commentary on the Old Testament (Eerdmans, 1994)

- David Prior, *The Message of Joel, Micah & Habakkuk*, The Bible Speaks Today (IVP, 1998)

KESWICK MINISTRIES

Our purpose

Keswick Ministries is committed to the spiritual renewal of God's people for his mission in the world.

God's purpose is to bring his blessing to all the nations of the world. That promise of blessing, which touches every aspect of human life, is ultimately fulfilled through the life, death, resurrection, ascension and future return of Christ. All of the people of God are called to participate in his missionary purposes, wherever he may place them. The central vision of Keswick Ministries is to see the people of God equipped, encouraged and refreshed to fulfil that calling, directed and guided by God's Word in the power of his Spirit, for the glory of his Son.

Our priorities

Keswick Ministries seeks to serve the local church through:

- *Hearing God's Word*: the Scriptures are the foundation for the church's life, growth and mission, and Keswick Ministries is committed to preaching and teaching God's Word in a way that is faithful to Scripture and relevant to Christians of all ages and backgrounds.

- *Becoming like God's Son*: from its earliest days the Keswick movement has encouraged Christians to live godly lives in the power of the Spirit, to grow in Christ-likeness and to live under his lordship in every area of life. This is God's will for his people in every culture and generation.

- *Serving God's mission*: the authentic response to God's Word is obedience to his mission, and the inevitable result of Christlikeness is sacrificial service. Keswick Ministries seeks to encourage committed discipleship in family life, work and society, and energetic engagement in the cause of world mission.

Our ministry

- *Keswick: the event.* Every summer the town of Keswick hosts a three-week convention, which attracts some 15,000 Christians from the UK and around the world. The event provides Bible teaching for all ages, vibrant worship, a sense of unity across generations and denominations, and an inspirational call to serve Christ in the world. It caters for children of all ages and has a strong youth and young adult programme. And it all takes place in the beautiful Lake District – a perfect setting for rest, recreation and refreshment.

- *Keswick: the movement.* For 140 years the work of Keswick has had an impact on churches worldwide, and today the movement is underway throughout the UK, as well as in many parts of Europe, Asia, North America, Australia, Africa and the Caribbean. Keswick Ministries is committed to strengthening the network in the UK and beyond, through prayer, news, pioneering and cooperative activity.

- *Keswick resources.* Keswick Ministries produces a range of books and booklets based on the core foundations of Christian life and mission. It makes Bible teaching available through free access to mp3 downloads, and the sale of DVDs and CDs. It broadcasts online through Clayton TV and annual BBC Radio 4 services.

- *Keswick teaching and training.* In addition to the summer convention, Keswick Ministries is developing teaching and training events that will happen at other times of the year and in other places.

Our unity

The Keswick movement worldwide has adopted a key Pauline statement to describe its gospel inclusivity: 'for you are all one in Christ Jesus' (Galatians 3:28). Keswick Ministries works with evangelicals from a wide variety of church backgrounds, on the understanding that they share a commitment to the essential truths of the Christian faith as set out in its statement of belief.

Our contact details
T: 01768 780075
E: info@keswickministries.org
W: www.keswickministries.org
Mail: Keswick Ministries, Rawnsley Centre, Main Street, Keswick, Cumbria CA12 5NP, England

Related titles from IVP

Food for the Journey

The Food for the Journey series offers daily devotionals from well-loved Bible teachers at the Keswick Convention in an ideal pocket-sized format – to accompany you wherever you go.

Available in the series

1 Thessalonians
Alec Motyer with
Elizabeth McQuoid
978 1 78359 439 9

Habakkuk
Jonathan Lamb with
Elizabeth McQuoid
978 1 78359 652 2

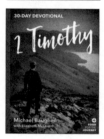

2 Timothy
Michael Baughen with
Elizabeth McQuoid
978 1 78359 438 2

Hebrews
Charles Price with
Elizabeth McQuoid
978 1 78359 611 9

Ezekiel
Liam Goligher with
Elizabeth McQuoid
978 1 78359 603 4

James
Stuart Briscoe with
Elizabeth McQuoid
978 1 78359 523 5

Available from your local Christian bookshop or **www.ivpbooks.com**

Food for the Journey

John 14 – 17
Simon Manchester with
Elizabeth McQuoid
978 1 78359 495 5

Ruth
Alistair Begg with
Elizabeth McQuoid
978 1 78359 525 9

Revelation
Paul Mallard with
Elizabeth McQuoid
978 1 78359 712 3

Praise for the series

'This devotional series is biblically rich, theologically deep and full of wisdom . . . I recommend it highly.' **Becky Manley Pippert, speaker, author of** *Out of the Saltshaker and into the World* **and creator of the Live/Grow/Know course and series of books**

'These devotional guides are excellent tools.' **John Risbridger, Minister and Team Leader, Above Bar Church, Southampton**

'These bite-sized banquets . . . reveal our loving Father weaving the loose and messy ends of our everyday lives into his beautiful, eternal purposes in Christ.' **Derek Burnside, Principal, Capernwray Bible School**

'I would highly recommend this series of 30-day devotional books to anyone seeking a tool that will help [him or her] to gain a greater love of scripture, or just simply . . . to do something out of devotion. Whatever your motivation, these little books are a must-read.' **Claud Jackson,** *Youthwork* **Magazine**

Available from your local Christian bookshop or **www.ivpbooks.com**

Related teaching CD and DVD packs

CD PACKS

1 Thessalonians
SWP2203D (5-CD pack)

2 Timothy
SWP2202D (4-CD pack)

Ezekiel
SWP2263D (5-CD pack)

Habakkuk
SWP2299D (5-CD pack)

Hebrews
SWP2281D (5-CD pack)

James
SWP2239D (4-CD pack)

John 14 – 17
SWP2238D (5-CD pack)

Revelation
SWP2300D (5-CD pack)

Ruth
SWP2280D (5-CD pack)

DVD PACKS

Ezekiel
SWP2263A (5-DVD pack)

Habakkuk
SWP2299A (5-DVD pack)

John 14 – 17
SWP2238A (5-DVD pack)

Revelation
SWP2300A (5-DVD pack)

Ruth
SWP2280A (5-DVD pack)

Available from www.essentialchristian.com